F/2/73
F/7/73

D1293483

PAMPHLETS ON AMERICAN WRITERS · NUMBER 93

UNIVERSITY OF MINNESOTA

Henry Adams

BY LOUIS AUCHINCLOSS

UNIVERSITY OF MINNESOTA PRESS · MINNEAPOLIS

Printed in the United States of America at
the North Central Publishing Company, St. Paul

Library of Congress Catalog Card Number: 70-633322
ISBN 0-8166-0596-3

PUBLISHED IN GREAT BRITAIN, INDIA, AND PAKISTAN BY THE OXFORD
UNIVERSITY PRESS, LONDON, BOMBAY, AND KARACHI, AND IN CANADA
BY THE COPP CLARK PUBLISHING CO. LIMITED, TORONTO

HENRY ADAMS

Louis Auchincloss is the author of many novels, short stories, and works of literary criticism. He has written two other pamphlets in this series, *Edith Wharton* and *Ellen Glasgow*, and the book *Pioneers and Caretakers: A Study of Nine American Women Novelists.*

↗ *Henry Adams*

ON DECEMBER 6, 1885, fate almost, in Henry Adams' words, "smashed the life" out of him. His wife, Marian Hooper Adams, on that day took a fatal dose of potassium cyanide. Suicide makes a clean sweep of the past and present; worst of all, it repudiates love. Adams was a man of few intimacies. "One friendship in a lifetime is much," he wrote; "two are many; three are hardly possible." Certainly his two were Clarence King, the geologist, and John Hay, the biographer of Lincoln. And there were others like the painter John La Farge with whom he had warm and pleasant associations. But it is doubtful if Adams, who used a sharp wit and a gruff, kindly cynicism as a barrier to and possibly a substitute for the closest human communion, ever revealed his deepest emotions or thoughts to any but Marian. She was quick, even caustic, but blessed with gaiety and an exquisite sensitivity. She adored her husband, and their childlessness was only a further bond. But nothing could pull her out of the black depression into which she sank after her father died.

Until that day of tragedy Henry Adams might have reasonably considered that his life was successful. He had not, to be sure, been president of the United States, like his grandfather, John Quincy Adams, or like his great-grandfather, John Adams, or minister to England, like his father, Charles Francis Adams, but he had been a brilliant and popular teacher of medieval history at Harvard, a successful editor of the *North American Review*, a noted biographer and essayist, and he was in the process of completing his nine-volume history of the Jefferson and Madison administrations which even such a self-deprecator as he must have suspected would one day be a classic. But above all this, far above, he had believed that he and his wife were happy.

Recovering from the first shock, he took a trip to Japan with John La Farge. Then he went back to Washington and worked for three laborious years to finish his history and prepare it for the press. After that, at last, he was free. He had neither child nor job, and his means were ample. In August of 1890 he and La Farge sailed again from San Francisco for a voyage of indefinite duration to the South Seas. His life, at fifty-two, seemed over. Like a worn-out race-horse, he had quit the course and was seeking pasture. "Education had ended in 1871, life was complete in 1890; the rest mattered so little!" And yet that rest was to contain the two great books for which Adams is chiefly remembered today: *Mont-Saint-Michel and Chartres* and *The Education of Henry Adams.*

The Pacific opened up a new dimension of color. La Farge taught Adams to observe the exquisite clearness of the butterfly blue of the sky, laid on between clouds and shading down to a white faintness in the distance where the haze of ocean covered up the turquoise. He made him peer down into the water, framed in the opening of a ship's gangway, and see how the sapphire blue seemed to pour from it. He pointed out the varieties of pink and lilac and purple and rose in the clouds at sunset. Adams never learned to be more than an amateur painter, but his vision was immensely sharpened. For the first time he began to allow the long-repressed aesthete, the author of two anonymous novels, to predominate over the intellectual, the historian.

In Samoa the natives, grave and courteous, greeted the travelers benevolently and made them feel at home. They drank the ceremonial *kawa* and watched the *siva*, a dance performed by girls seated cross-legged, naked to the waist, their dark skins shining with coconut oil, with garlands of green leaves around their heads and loins. The girls chanted as they swayed and stretched out their arms

6

in all directions; they might have come out of the nearby sea. It was a world where instinct was everything.

After Samoa came the disillusionment of Tahiti. Adams described it as a successful cemetery. The atmosphere was one of hopelessness and premature decay. The natives were not the gay, big animal creatures of Samoa; they were still, silent, sad in expression, and fearfully few in number. The population had been decimated by bacteria brought in by Westerners. Rum was the only amusement which civilization and religion had left the people. Tahiti was a halfway house between Hawaii and Samoa. Adams complained that a pervasive half-castitude permeated everything, a sickly whitey-brown or dirty white complexion that suggested weakness and disease.

He was bored, bored as he had never been in the worst wilds of Beacon Street or at the dreariest dinner tables of Belgravia. While waiting for a boat to take them elsewhere, anywhere, he amused himself by returning to his role of historian and interviewing members of the deposed royal family, the Tevas. Next to Mataafa in Samoa, he found the old ex-queen of Tahiti, Hinari, or Grandmother, the most interesting native figure in the Pacific. She showed none of the secrecy of the Samoan chiefs, but took a motherly interest in Adams and La Farge and, sitting on the floor, told them freely all her clan's oldest legends and traditions. Adams was even adopted into the Teva clan and given the hereditary family name of Taura-Atua with the lands, rights, and privileges attached to it — though these consisted of only a few hundred square feet.

But later when he attempted to recapture Hinari's tale in a book which he had privately printed, it was little more than an interesting failure. Tahiti had no history, in the Western sense of the word, until the arrival of the white man. Of the thousands of years that had preceded Captain Cook, when generation had succeeded generation without distinguishable change, there was nothing left but

7

genealogy and legend. The genealogy, which makes up a large part of Adams' book, is boring, and, as for the legend, he admitted himself that he needed the lighter hand of Robert Louis Stevenson, whom he had met in Tahiti.

Yet *The Memoirs of Arii Taimai* (1901) nonetheless marks an important step in Adams' career. He had gone, by 1890, as far as he could go as a historian in the conventional sense. His great work on Jefferson and Madison was history at its most intellectually pure. The author stands aside and lets the documents tell the story, from which a few precious rules may be deduced. In the South Seas he had tried to abandon intellect for the sake of simplicity and instinct. He had sought peace and found ennui. Even the unspoiled natives, in the long run, palled. He had to return, in Papeete, to his profession, but he had to try it with a new twist, for how else could Tahitian history be done? And if *The Memoirs* was a bore, was it altogether his fault? Might it not be in the subject? Suppose he were to happen upon a subject that required not only the imagination of the man who had sat on the floor with the old queen of Tahiti as she intoned the poems of her family tradition, but also the industry of the devoted scholar who had pored through the archives of European foreign offices? Suppose he were to find a subject, in short, that required an artist as well as a historian? A subject like the Gothic age of faith?

To go back to his origin (as he himself so often did), Adams was born in Boston in 1838, in Mount Vernon Street under the shadow of the State House. He always loved to dramatize the irony of the seemingly fortunate circumstances of his birth. According to his claim, he had been less equipped for life in America in the nineteenth century than had he been born a Polish Jew or "a furtive Yacoob and Ysaac still reeking of the Ghetto, snarling a weird Yiddish to the officers of the customs." The notion is not to be taken

8

too seriously. If Adams was aloof from the political and economic competition of his day it was not because he was the grandson of a president and, on his mother's side, of the richest merchant in Boston. It was quite of his own volition. Had he been born obscure the idea would never have occurred to him, as an old and respected seer, that he was a failure.

From earliest childhood he was close to the great. When he refused to go to school, it was old John Quincy Adams himself who took him by the hand and led him there. When he went to church, it was to sleep through the sermons of his uncle, Nathaniel Frothingham. Studying his Latin grammar in a corner of his father's library in Mount Vernon Street he heard Charles Sumner hold forth on the politics of antislavery, and at the age of twelve he was taken to Washington to call on President Zachary Taylor and the leaders of Congress. The pattern of receiving his impressions of current history from the very apex of the political pyramid was to continue for the rest of a long life.

He grew up in a large and happy family of six children, two girls and four boys, with devoted parents who were always close to them. He attended the Dixwell School in Boston and entered Harvard College in 1854. When he graduated, four years later, he was elected class orator. Although he always maintained that he learned nothing at Cambridge, this was part of an affectation that covered every stage of his life. In fact, he seems to have read widely, obtained good grades, and made friends with classmates who were also to make their mark in life. One was Henry Hobson Richardson, the Romanesque architect who later built Adams' house in Washington; another was Oliver Wendell Holmes, Jr., of the Supreme Court. Adams' class oration contained none of the pessimism for which he was afterwards noted, and his Class Book has this entry under his signature: "My immediate object is to become a scholar, and master of more languages than I pretend to know now.

9

Ultimately it is most probable that I shall study and practise law, but where and to what extent is as yet undecided. My wishes are for a quiet literary life, as I believe that to be the happiest and in this country not the least useful." This should rebut those who claim that Adams abandoned public life in later years because he disliked the rough and tumble of competition. At twenty he had already elected to be a writer.

After graduation he spent two years in Europe. His original purpose had been to study German civil law in Berlin, but he found it hopelessly boring and decided to learn only the language. Ultimately his trip turned, more profitably, into a sort of grand tour. In Sicily he had an interview with Garibaldi, and in Rome he sat, like Gibbon, on the top of the steps to Santa Maria di Ara Coeli and mused over the great work of history that that historian had visualized on the same spot. When he returned to Boston, he was still determined to read for the bar, but he was interrupted again — this time by his father's election to Congress and the latter's proposal that he accompany him to Washington as private secretary.

Adams remained his father's secretary for nine years, from 1860 to 1868. It was the nearest he ever came to public office. After a brief time in a capital seething with secession, Charles Francis Adams was sent to London as minister. He occupied this position brilliantly and successfully throughout the Civil War and during the difficult period of the adjustment of war claims that followed. There is little reason to believe that his son felt estranged from his generation — as did his friend Henry James — by not having seen combat. Adams knew that his father, supported by a tiny staff, was fighting a battle against British Confederate sympathies that was quite as vital as any in the field, and his older brother warned him sternly from his army camp that if Henry left his post to enlist he would be derelict in his duty to both family and nation. There was no feeling on anyone's part that the little isolated Union group in

London was having an easy time. Adams was perfectly sincere in his belief that combat, under the circumstances, would have come as a relief.

But whatever the pressures during crises, there must have been periods, in the more leisurely diplomatic life of that era, when there was not enough to do, for Adams in these years traveled all over England and began to write. He gave considerable attention to a piece on John Smith and Pocahontas, ultimately published in the *North American Review*, in which he was able to disprove some of the foundations on which that flimsy legend rested. Why he took this article, then and later, so seriously is hard to see. He seemed to think, a bit naively, that it might upset those British aristocrats who claimed descent from the Indian princess. At any rate, it is only interesting today as his first serious historical work and because it shows his method, developed more skillfully later, of letting the quoted documents tell most of the story.

When the war ended, he continued to write solid, scholarly articles, such as "The Declaration of Paris" and "The Bank of England Restriction," but it was not until his return to live in Washington as a free-lance correspondent that his distinctive style and point of view began to appear. It took anger and disgust to bring this out: the anger and disgust that was felt by thousands of idealistic young men who saw what they had hoped would be the brave new world of an emancipated and now indissoluble union turned over to a gang of ward politicians and economic pirates. Abraham Lincoln was dead, and Jay Gould seemed to reign at the White House.

"The New York Gold Conspiracy," dealing with the attempt of Gould and Fisk to corner the gold market with the aid of President Grant's brother-in-law, is a fine, taut narrative that crackles with the author's contempt for the crooks and dupes of the sordid adventure. Adams had by now completed his mastery of finance, and

11

his exposition is as clear as it is eloquent. "The Legal Tender Act," about the sorry federal financing of 1862, and "The Session," about the congressional session of 1869–70, are in much the same vein. But the world was not interested in the lucid diagnoses of this brilliant thirty-two-year-old reformer. The world cared about votes and dollars, and Adams lacked the temperament needed to acquire the first and the greed for the second. Besides, he was well enough off, not rich, by the standards of Wall Street, but able to make himself completely comfortable. Adams was always to live rather exquisitely; he was at heart a bit of a sybarite. In his old age this was to make his pretenses of being an anarchist seem an occasionally tiresome parlor joke to younger observers.

In 1870 his life changed again when Charles W. Eliot offered him the post of assistant professor of medieval history at Harvard. Characteristically, Adams told Eliot that he knew nothing about medieval history. Characteristically, Eliot responded by offering to appoint anyone who, in Adams' opinion, knew more. He held the job for seven years during which he also held the editorship of the *North American Review*. His classes were small and select, and his students were turned loose to forage for themselves in original source material. Adams worked with them, rather than over them. He called the experiment a failure in *The Education*, but his students remembered the course as an inspiring one. One class even wrote and published a book under his direction, *Essays in Anglo-Saxon Law*. One may doubt that Adams, at the time, really believed that this was failure.

At any rate, he gave up both teaching and editing before he was forty. He and his wife, Marian Hooper of Boston, whom he had married in 1872, settled in Washington, and he began at last a full-time career as a historian. The next eight years were the happiest of his life. The young Adamses were the center of the brightest, gayest group in the capital. Henry James was to describe them at this period with good-natured sharpness in the guise of the Alfred Bonnycastles in "Pandora." Mrs. Bonnycastle in that tale has a fund of good humor that is apt to come uppermost with the April blossoms; her husband is "not in politics, though politics were much in him." They solve their social problems simply by not knowing any of the people they do not want to know, although here Mr. Bonnycastle sometimes finds his wife a bit too choosy. He remarks toward the end of the season: "Hang it, there's only a month left, let us be vulgar and have some fun — let us invite the President!"

But with all the fun and the parties Adams was still hard at work. He had acquired the Albert Gallatin papers which he edited in three large volumes, with a fourth for his own biography of Jefferson's secretary of the treasury (1879). As history the life is admirable; as entertainment it is very dry. One doubts if even such a literary magician as Lytton Strachey could have made Gallatin's personality interesting. However high-minded, judicious, industrious, patriotic, conscientious, Gallatin was dull and his correspondence is dull, and dullness permeates his biography. Adams demonstrates all of his subject's best qualities in his own careful, clear rendition of the important facts, and there they remain for students, and for students only.

Just the opposite is true of Adams' biography of John Randolph of Roanoke (1882). Here he is dealing with an absolutely reprehensible man who was the scourge of the House of Representatives for two decades and who ultimately came to symbolize everything that was violent, recalcitrant, and irrational in the point of view of the southern slaveholder. Randolph's importance in history is that he became the prophet around whom the forces of secession could ultimately rally. It is certain that he was alcoholic; it is probable that he was partially insane. No more different character from Gallatin could possibly be conceived, and they face each other a little bit like Milton's God and Milton's Satan, with the balance of interest falling in Satan's favor. Fortunately, the book on Randolph is short, for about halfway through one begins to lose interest. The character is too absurd to hold the stage except as a grisly historical fact, and once that historical fact has been set forth there is little to be gained by summaries of his irrational speeches. The work ultimately fails, like *Gallatin*, because of its subject. It could have only been strengthened if Adams had had the material and the inclination to delve into the psychological reasons for Randolph's behavior. He would have done better to have made it the topic of one of his masterly essays in the *North American Review*. As he said himself, Randolph's biographer had the impossible job of taking a "lunatic monkey" seriously.

Gallatin and Randolph were both to play major roles in the great historical work on which Adams now embarked: *The History of the United States of America during the Administrations of Thomas Jefferson and James Madison*. When completed it ran to nine volumes, the last of which was not published until 1891. Before the appearance of Dumas Malone's study of Jefferson's first term, Adams' *History* was considered by many the definitive work on the first years of the American nineteenth century.

The short chapters, the straightforward, vigorous, masculine prose, the geographical and political sweep of the narrative, and the sharp, pungent assessments of motives and failings, conceal the enormous and laborious research in American, French, English, and Spanish state papers that underlay them. Adams was to say in *The Education* that he had published a dozen volumes of American history for no other purpose than to satisfy himself whether, by the severest process of stating, with the least possible comment, such facts as seemed sure, in such order as seemed rigorously consequent, he could fix for a familiar moment a necessary sequence of human movement. He selected his period (1801 to 1817) because it represented a natural semicolon in American history. By the turn of the century the United States had established itself as an independent nation that was bound, one way or another, to survive, and by 1815 that nation had accepted the fact, whether all of its statesmen did so or not, that it was going to survive more or less as other nations survived. It was not, in other words, to be an Arcadia — set apart. The two double terms of Jefferson and Madison represent, therefore, the historical hiatus in which Americans gave up their dream that they were different from other human beings. Adams' central theme is the disillusionment of two presidents who found that their governments were ineluctably controlled by facts and not ideals.

Both presidents were to find themselves in the position of Napoleon in Tolstoi's *War and Peace*, pulling at tassels inside a carriage under the illusion that it was they, rather than the charging horses, who made it go. Adams demonstrates that when history offered Jefferson the chance to purchase Louisiana, he discovered that he could not turn it down — that he did not even want to. So he doubled the size of the union by means of a treaty for which there was no shadow of authority in the Constitution whose strict construction he had so passionately urged. And Madison, in his turn, according to Adams, found himself obliged to build up the armed forces that he had wished to abolish and to engage in warfare which he had believed fatal to liberty. And both he and Jefferson found themselves caught up in the job of enforcing an embargo as despotically as any tyrant abroad.

This conception of Jefferson as an idealist philosopher-president, imbued with the fatuous faith that there were no international difficulties that could not be solved by negotiation, has been subject to the criticism that Adams was prejudiced against the third president, who, after spurning the political ideas of John Adams, ended by adopting them. There may be some truth in this. Why should

Adams attack Jefferson for inconsistency, which can be a very great virtue in a statesman, unless he believed that the latter had pre-empted a credit in history that more properly belonged to his great-grandfather? Then, too, Adams, with the down-to-earth thinking of the scholar who has never been tempted to compromise, may have found it difficult to appreciate the enormous range and flexibility of Jefferson's political mind. Adams admired diplomats and rarely politicians. Jefferson was rarely a diplomat and always a politician. One is reminded at times of Lord Morley's statement that if Adams had ever surveyed himself naked in a mirror, he might have been more tolerant of human deficiencies.

Adams' predilection for diplomacy is the source of the best and weakest parts of the *History*. The more brilliant passages are those that take place outside the United States: in London, Paris, and Madrid; in St. Domingo and on the high seas. The chapters that deal with Napoleon have a particular fascination, not only because they put the naive, serious-minded American statesmen in dramatic contrast with this monster of Old World cynicism and champion of brute force, but because they show Adams, the historian, struggling desperately in his quest for sequence, for cause and effect, against the tide of chaos, against the appalling evidence that a single individual was turning history into whim. Napoleon plays in the *History* just the reverse of the role that he plays in *War and Peace*. It is ironical that Adams, who largely agreed with Tolstoi's concept of political leaders being carried along in the flood of events which they try vainly to control, should take exception to Tolstoi's primary illustration of his theory. Yet so it is. Napoleon seems to strike Adams as the one human being of the period who contains in himself an energy equivalent to a nation's energy and who is thus able to deflect history from its normal course. When one sees the emperor lolling in his hot bath and shouting at his brothers about the Louisiana Purchase, one feels that Adams is here dealing with a different kind of force from that generated by Jefferson, by Burr, by Canning, or even by Andrew Jackson. The mere fact that Napoleon is the only man in nine volumes whom we see in a bathtub underlines his individuality. Eventually, the processes of history would right themselves, and Napoleon's empire would disintegrate, even more quickly than it was put together, but it still remains a phenomenon unique in European history.

One can see why Adams was ultimately disappointed in his sequences. For despite all his labors and all his perceptions, the true cause of the War of 1812 is never made clear. Through several volumes of lucidly described diplomatic negotiations between England and the United States we see the government first of Jefferson and then of Madison submit tamely to every humiliation imposed upon it by a British crown determined not only to keep its former colony a small power but to seize by any means, legal or illegal, its growing trade. Adams pursues skillfully, if at times tediously, the endless negotiations in the seven years preceding the war: in Paris, Washington, and London, over the American embargo, the American Act of Non-Intercourse, the British Orders in Council, and Napoleon's Berlin and Milan decrees. Fixed in the policy of isolation, hallucinated by the vision that the new democracy, left to itself, would develop powerfully and peacefully, Jefferson and his successor are seen deliberately blinding themselves to the fact that neither Canning nor Napoleon will give the slightest consideration to any diplomatic protest that is not backed up by force.

But why then the war? Why did the United States, having suffered every diplomatic rebuff, finally elect to throw away the price of its shameful submission? So far as the reader can make out, the country was hounded unprepared into a war which its administration did not seek by a group of young hotheads in Congress led by Henry Clay and John C. Calhoun. But Adams did not know why: "The war fever of 1811 swept far and wide over the country, but even at its height seemed somewhat intermittent and imaginary. A passion that needed to be nursed for five years before it acquired strength to break into act, could not seem genuine to men who did not share it. A nation which had submitted to robbery and violence in 1805, in 1807, in 1809, could not readily lash itself into rage in 1811 when it had no new grievance to allege; nor could the public feel earnest in maintaining national honor, for every one admitted that the nation had sacrificed its honor, and must fight to regain it. Yet what honor was to be hoped from a war which required continued submission to one robber as the price of resistance to another? President Madison submitted to Napoleon in order to resist England; the New England Federalists preferred submitting to England in order to resist Napoleon; but not one American expected the United States to uphold their national rights against the world."

It is difficult for the reader at this point not to ask why, if a war is going to be created simply by an unreasonable war fever, such an inordinate amount of space has been devoted to the unraveling of the diplomatic skein that is not directly related to it. Of course, it might be answered that the unraveling of the diplomatic skein is part of a historian's task simply because it is there to unravel, but even conceding this, one cannot escape the conclusion that the diplomatic chapters could be summarized without losing much of their importance. One suspects here that Adams, being a pioneer in the British, French, and Spanish archives, fell a little bit in love with material so far virgin to the historian and indulged in overquotation. There is also the fact that, having himself spent eight years as secretary to the United States minister in London, he had a natural fascination in peering under the formal cover of diplomatic interchange to the reality beneath.

Adams believed that a historian should first detach himself and his personal enthusiasms and disapprovals from the field of human events that he has selected to study. He should then develop his own general ideas of causes and effects by observing the mass of phenomena in the selected period. After the formation of such ideas, he should exclude all facts irrelevant to them. In his *History*, his most important general idea is that the energy of the American people ultimately seized control of a chain of events which was initiated by energies in Europe. He attempted to trace this American energy in finance, science, politics, and diplomacy. Individuals were not of primary importance to him, which explains why even Jefferson is never presented in a full portrait and why Madison remains a more shadowy character than any of the British statesmen described. Adams believed that in a democratic nation individuals were important chiefly as types. In the end, his *History*, like most great histories, is a failure, if a splendid one, because we are never brought to a full comprehension of what this all-important energy consists. It seems possible that Adams might have approached its nature more closely had he widened his field of study, had he spent more time observing the commercial society of American cities, the farms of the North and the plantations in the South, and less of the day-to-day negotiations of the Treaty of Ghent.

During the years of heavy work on his *History*, Adams relaxed from one discipline, characteristically, by subjecting himself to another. He wrote and published two novels, *Democracy*, which appeared anonymously in 1880, and *Esther*, which he brought out under the pseudonym of Frances Snow Compton in 1884. The identity of the author was for years a carefully guarded secret. These novels have aroused an interest in our time incommensurate with their merit. They are in the class of Winston Churchill's paintings — of primary interest to the biographer. That is not to say that they are bad. Indeed, competently organized and agreeably written, they cause no squirms of embarrassment even to the most critical reader. But compared to Adams' other work they are pale stuff, and commentators are reduced to the scholar's game of spotting the origins of the *Education* in *Democracy* and that of *Mont-Saint-Michel and Chartres* in *Esther*. Mrs. Lightfoot Lee's disenchantment with her corrupt senator, exposed by Adams' alter ego, John Carrington, reflects the author's own disgust with post-Civil War Washington, and Esther Dudley's rejection of the Episcopal Church contains the seed of Adams' nostalgia for a church that she might not have rejected. Yet neither novel significantly illuminates the later works. They remain in the end footnotes for Adams enthusiasts.

Democracy attained considerable popularity in its day as a political roman à clef. Certainly, the characters are more subtle than the issues. Mrs. Lightfoot Lee, like a Jamesian heroine, has money and social position and a bright, fresh spirit full of ideals. She has come to Washington in quest of some great and enlightened statesman whose humble and helping consort she may become. Her cousin John Carrington falls in love with her, but he is not at all what she wants. He is a Confederate veteran who has lost all and accepted defeat, but only because he has grimly accepted the verdict of history. Despising the victors, he concentrates on making a lonely living as a lawyer in the conquerors' land, a cynical, trenchant, attractive figure, the only real man in the book, so much like Basil Ransom in Henry James's novel *The Bostonians* of the same period that one wonders if he and Adams might not have used the same model.

Madeleine Lee wants something much more effervescent than Carrington; he is cold tea to the champagne that she visualizes. At last she thinks that she has found her ideal in Senator Ratcliffe, the colossus of Illinois who is able to gain control of the administration of the new president before the latter has even taken office. It is Carrington's distasteful duty to disillusion Madeleine, and he resolutely goes about putting together the necessary proof that the senator's career has been founded on a bribe. Madeleine, convinced, flees both senator and Washington. That is the whole story.

It is flat. One might have hoped that Madeleine would at least fall in love with the villain — if only to make her decision harder — but her creator, who detested senators, could not allow this. One might also have hoped that the senator would devise an interesting defense to her charge. But he tells Madeleine that the end justifies the means, and his end is nothing but the tired old rhetorical goal used by every contemporary statesman who ever waved the bloody shirt: preservation of the union. Adams might have answered this criticism of his plot by pointing out that he was telling the simple truth. Statesmen like Senator Ratcliffe in the reconstruction era *did* dominate the scene, and men like Carrington *were* helpless to do more than record their own indignant dissent. Madeleine Lee, in flying off to Europe, has only expressed the despair of her creator at the prospect of Washington. Living a century later in not dissimilar times, should we not appreciate her position? Perhaps. But we are dealing with a novel, and novels must be concerned less with truth than the appearance of it.

Esther Dudley's choice in *Esther* is a good deal harder than Madeleine's, for she is very much in love. The story again involves a renunciation, her renunciation of a deeply religious young minister whose faith she finds she cannot share. The novel is full of their arguments and finally bogs down in the reader's inability to see why an agnostic, with a little bit of tact, could not be a perfectly good minister's wife. One is almost surprised, in the end, that the subject has not been more interesting. It cannot be only that we care less about the question of faith today. Our interest in *Anna Karenina* is not diminished by our knowing that today the heroine could have divorced her husband and married Vronski with no loss of social position. No, it is rather that Adams himself has so little

21

sympathy for the Reverend Stephen Hazard. He makes his evan-
gelicism ridiculous, so that one suspects that Esther may be well
out of her engagement. If the man of political power in the 1870's
and 1880's was a pirate, the man of God was an anachronism. As
husbands went, there was not much to choose between them. Esther
would have to wait twenty years and visit Chartres Cathedral, as
one of Adams' adopted nieces, before she would encounter a religion that could move the hearts of men. And even then it would
only be the memory of one.

There is a distinct similarity between Adams' two heroines and
the heroines of Henry James's early and middle periods. Madeleine and Esther each have the impulsiveness, the charm, and the
strict integrity of Isabel Archer in *The Portrait of a Lady*. It is
probable that this freshness and ebullience, this happy idealism
united with a stubborn, at times gooselike, refusal to compromise,
was a characteristic of American girls of the period and perhaps of
Marian Adams herself. It was what made them ultimately pathetic,
at times even tragic. One can find analogies in the American girls
of Anthony Trollope's later novels. But certainly with Adams
himself, this concept reflects a deep preoccupation. All his life he
was more at ease with women than men, and after Marian's death
he transferred some of his dependence to Elizabeth Cameron, the
beautiful wife of Senator Don Cameron of Pennsylvania. When he
wrote Mrs. Cameron that he valued any dozen pages of *Esther*
more than the whole of his *History*, he may have been only half
serious, but he may also have been expressing an intuitive conviction that the charm of Esther Dudley was precisely what was
missing from the historical work.

Esther was Adams' last publication before his wife's suicide, and
the years that followed, as we have seen, were occupied with the
laborious completion of the *History*. His winters were now spent
in the house designed for him by Henry Hobson Richardson on

Lafayette Square directly opposite the White House. The adjoining larger mansion, also designed by Richardson, belonged to the John Hays. Adams had given up going out socially, but he continued to entertain a select number of friends for lunch, or what he called breakfast. In the other seasons he traveled: in the Pacific, in the Caribbean, in Europe, in the Middle East. He had ceased to consider himself a historian. He was simply a student of the universe, an asker of questions, a humble seeker after knowledge who hoped to have a peek into the essential nature of man and matter before he died. This picture of a small, gruff gentleman, poking about the planet and asking questions of every sphinx, is the character, of course, that he himself was to make the subject of *The Education of Henry Adams.*

Among Adams' intimates was Senator Henry Cabot Lodge of Massachusetts who had been one of his students at Harvard. The friendship at times was a rather prickly one, since Adams tended to distrust senators in general and Lodge in particular, but with Mrs. Lodge, a woman of large sympathy and intellect, the relationship was always good. It was she who invited him on the tour of northern France in the summer of 1895 which first aroused his interest in Norman and Gothic cathedrals. In the Cathedral of Coutances he suddenly saw his ideal image of outward austerity and inward refinement and felt a consequent release from the era in which he had been condemned to live. From this point on he began to play a mental game in which he identified himself with his Norman ancestors.

It did not matter whether these had been peasants or princes. All classes, in the eleventh century, must have felt the same motives. It had been, as Adams saw it, a natural, reasonable, complete century in which to live. Its cathedrals showed neither extravagance nor want of practical sense. He could almost remember the faith that had given his ancestors the energy to build them and the scared boldness that had made their towers seem so daring. Within these citadels of faith no doubts existed. There was not a stone in the whole interior of Coutances that did not treat him as if he were its own child. Going back eight hundred years, he mused: "I was simple-minded, somewhat stiff and cold, almost repellent to the warmer natures of the south, and I had lived always where one fought handily and needed to defend ones wives and children; but I was at my best." The fatal mistake had been ever to conquer England and its "dull, beer-swilling people." From 1066 to the Boston of Adams' own childhood, there had been nothing but a long decline in religion, in art, in military taste, until now, in the summer of 1895, the Back Bay descendants of Caen and Coutances had pretty nearly reached bottom.

In Mont-Saint-Michel the party encountered large numbers of tourists. Adams described them petulantly as pigs and the meals that he had to eat as hogpens. He does not seem to have run into many tourists in the other places, and one shudders to think what his reaction would have been had he traveled today. What struck him most in the Mount was that its character was more military than religious. He was fascinated by Senator Lodge's enthusiasm for it. Adams had not anticipated much from his friend as a sight-seer. Lodge, he had been afraid, would visit the dreary old capitals of Europe as though he was still twenty and as though Napoleon III was still reigning. Now, however, Lodge returned to the enthusiasm that he had manifested as a student under Adams at Harvard, and lectured the party brilliantly on the construction and fortifications of the monastery.

The climax of the trip came with Chartres. After "thirty-five years of postponed intentions," Adams worshiped at last before the splendor of "the great glass gods." For the first time he encountered something that even his critical mind could regard as perfection. It was an experience that he was never to get over. He divined in the cathedral the intention of twelfth-century man to unite all arts and sciences in the service of God. It was an architectural exhibit, a museum of painting, glass staining, wood and stone carving, music (vocal and instrumental), embroidery, jewelry, gem setting, tapestry weaving. It was the greatest single creation of man, to whom it gave a dignity which he was in no other instances entitled to claim. Adams likened himself to a monkey looking through a telescope at the stars.

Chartres was a beautiful gate by which to leave his Norman paradise, but he could hardly bear to leave it. The chateaux of the Loire seemed now as vulgar as Newport. Valois art was a "Jewish kind of gold-bug style" best fitted to express the coarseness and sensuality of Francis I and Henry VIII and their unspeakable Field of the Cloth of Gold. And when Adams returned to Paris, it was even worse. He was sickened by the "dreadful twang of his dear country people" on the Rue de la Paix. But people did not so much matter so long as one had the Gothic cathedrals.

After his trip with the Lodges Adams returned every summer to Paris. He rented an apartment as a base for his excursions and always invited a niece or nieces to visit him. Friends of nieces were also welcome, and "Uncle Henry" became a cult, the adored center of a group of attractive and intelligent young women. He would usually take one or more with him on his motor trips in search of the twelfth and thirteenth centuries. By the summer of 1904 he wrote to John Hay that these expeditions had become a craze and that he had fallen a victim to his Mercedes. He spent the warm months running "madly through the centuries" hunting "windows like hairs," covering sixty miles in a morning and ninety in an afternoon. Traveling down a straight French road through the countryside hypnotized him "as a chalk line does a hen." He gathered the fruit of these excursions into the volume which he entitled *Mont-Saint-Michel and Chartres*.

It has always been a difficult book for librarians to classify. Should it be catalogued under travel or history or even fiction? Certainly, it purports to pass in the first category. The narrator claims that he is writing a guidebook for a niece, adoptive or actual, on a long, leisurely summer tourist trip from Brittany to Paris to Chartres. The point of view from which we take the story is the uncle's. He, of course, is Adams himself, a first-class traveler, as selective in his scholarship as he undoubtedly is in his foods and wines, with nothing to interrupt him in a happy season of poking about in Gothic cathedrals. The atmosphere of the golden age of tourism pervades the story. A generation before, and travel was all dusty roads, jolting carriages, and pot-luck inns. A few years later it would be the sharing of treasures with a million seekers and a thousand buses. But just at the turn of the century, with the advent of the automobile, for a brief delectable time, the past belonged to a few happy exquisites, who wrote big illustrated volumes such as Henry James's *Italian Hours* and Edith Wharton's *A Motor Flight through France*. The "pigs" whom Adams had seen in Brittany were easily avoided.

The reader of *Mont-Saint-Michel* soon learns that he is in the hands of no ordinary guide. The uncle disclaims any pretensions of being an architect, a historian, or a theologian; he insists on only one virtue, an indispensable one in any honest tourist: he is "seriously interested in putting the feeling back into the dead architecture where it belongs." That he succeeds in this I think no reader will dispute. Whether it is always the appropriate feeling may sometimes be in question. When it is, Adams is a great historian. When it is not, he is a great romantic.

We start in the eleventh century at Mont-Saint-Michel in Brittany just before the Norman Conquest of England. Adams' architectural plot begins with the Romanesque, the rounded arch, the age of the conquering soldier and militant priest, of the Chanson de Roland, an age of simple, serious, silent dignity and tremendous energy. We move through Caen to Paris and at last to Chartres and the year 1200, the time of the Gothic arch and the cult of the Virgin. This Adams sees as the finest and most intense moment of the Christian story. The chapters on the Cathedral of Chartres, on its statuary, its apses, its incomparable glass, are a remarkable lyrical achievement. Adams sees Mary as superior to the Trinity. She is what equity is to law. There is no hope for sinful men in the rigid, logical justice of Christ. He is law, unity, perfection, a closed system. But the Virgin is a woman, loving, capricious, kind, infinitely merciful. She is nature, love, chaos. The cathedral is her palace, and the most beautiful art in history is displayed there to please her. Adams makes us feel at one with the crushed crowd of kneeling twelfth-century worshipers as we lift our eyes after the miracle of the Mass to see, far above the high altar, "high over all the agitation of prayer, the passion of politics, the anguish of suffering, the terrors of sin, only the figure of the Virgin in majesty." But the chapter ends on a dry note. Moving suddenly back to his own day the uncle leaves the Virgin "looking down from a deserted heaven, into an empty church, on a dead faith."

That is the end of the architectural trip, yet the book is only half finished. Adams now traces the influence of the Virgin in literature, in contemporary history, and in theology. He offers translations of some of the versifications of her miracles; he describes the great royal ladies of the period; he conveys the sense of Mary's ambience in the world of court poems and courteous love. The emotion in these chapters begins to approach that of the naive and passionate chroniclers whom he quotes. He sternly warns us that if we do not appreciate the charm of this or that, we may as well give up trying to understand the age. Our guide has become a priest and one of Mary's own. The feeling conveyed is a unique aesthetic effect.

He does not, however, leave us in the days of Mariolatry. The priest now turns professor. In the last chapters he explains how the church was taken away from the Virgin. She was a heretic, in essence, for she denied the authority of God and asserted the greater force of woman. The theologians had to put her back in her place and build a religious philosophy that would stand up to the most unsettling questions of the logicians. In the final chapter on St. Thomas Aquinas Adams sees him building his theology as men built cathedrals: "Knowing by an enormous experience precisely where the strains were to come, they enlarged their scale to the utmost point of material endurance, lightening the load and distributing the burden until the gutters and gargoyles that seem mere ornament, and the grotesques that seem rude absurdities, all do work either for the arch or for the eye; and every inch of material, up and down, from crypt to vault, from man to God, from the universe to the atom, had its task, giving support where support was needed, or weight where concentration was felt, but always with the condition of showing conspicuously to the eye the great lines which led to unity and the curves which controlled divergence; so that, from the cross on the flèche and the keystone of the vault, down through the ribbed nervures, the columns, the windows, to the foundation of the flying buttresses far beyond the walls, one idea controlled every line; and this is true of Saint Thomas's Church as it is of Amiens Cathedral. The method was the same for both, and the result was an art marked by singular unity, which endured and served its purpose until man changed his attitude toward the universe. . . . Granted a Church, Saint Thomas's Church was the most expressive that man has made, and the great Gothic cathedrals were its most complete expression."

Is it true? Was France like that in the twelfth and thirteenth centuries? It has often been pointed out that Adams' idyllic era of true faith was actually a period of lawless strife and brigandage in which a few ambitious and secular-minded priests raised cathedrals to their own glory. Undoubtedly he oversimplified, exaggerated. His Chartres may be to cathedrals as Moby Dick is to whales. But if the religious spirit that he so brilliantly evokes in his strong sinuous prose did in fact exist, he may, by isolating it from the turmoil in which it was embedded, have come closer to the essence of his era than some more comprehensive historians.

How far Adams has traveled in his experiments with historical method may be measured by contrasting his *Gallatin* with *Mont-Saint-Michel*. The former shows the historian at his most restrained. The documents speak for the author, while in the latter the historian (or guide) propels us despotically by the elbow, allowing us to see only what appeals to his own taste (at times almost his whim), and colors the whole panorama with his violent personal distaste for his own times. But the guide is always entertaining, and the reader, one submits, may know Eleanor of Guienne and Abélard better than, in the earlier works, he knows any member of Jefferson's cabinet.

At this period of Adams' life he was close to political power for the first time. He had always been close enough to observe it, but now he was in a position, if not to exercise it, at least to influence its exercise. John Hay, his most intimate friend, his soul's brother, was Theodore Roosevelt's secretary of state. Might Adams not be a Gray Eminence? He had always maintained that a friend in power was a friend lost, but this cynical observation had to be modified to except the case of Hay whose gentle, affectionate, and loyal disposition was proof against all strains of high political life. Also, Hay was an ill man who held on to the office which finally killed him only at the promptings of duty. A necessary relaxation was his daily walk with Adams, after which Mrs. Hay would give them tea. If Adams, according to Hay, could "growl and tease" in "hours of ease," he could also be a "ministering angel" in times of anguish. When Hay died, still in office, in the summer of 1905, Adams wrote to his widow: "As for me, it is time to bid good-bye. I am tired. My last hold on the world is lost with him. I can no longer look a month ahead, or be sure of my hand or mind. I have hung on to his activities till now because they were his, but except as his they have no concern for me and I have no more strength for them . . . He and I began life together. We will stop together."

The exaggeration was characteristic. Adams had another thirteen years to live, and he was already at work on his most famous book. He had planned the *Education* as a companion piece to *Mont-Saint-Michel*. It would present the twentieth century in contrast to the twelfth: the chaos of infinite multiplicity as opposed to Saint Thomas Aquinas' divine order. Adams had been fascinated at the Paris Exposition of 1900 by the Gallery of Machines of the Champ de Mars. This he had visited day after day to watch in entrancement the silent whirring of the great dynamos. He wrote to Hay that they ran as noiselessly and as smoothly as the planets and that he wanted to ask them, with infinite courtesy, where the hell they were going. He saw in them the tremendous, ineluctable force of science in the new century. Surely, it was the very opposite of the warm concept of the overwatching Virgin of Chartres. As his new book came to mind, it may have occurred to him in that very gallery that the narrator who would constitute the most dramatic contrast to the dynamo would be the one who was then watching it: Henry Adams himself.

He may also have been induced to put the book in the form of a memoir (in the third person) by two other factors: first, his dislike of biographies in general, coupled with the fear that he himself might one day be the victim of a hack, and, second, by his enthusiasm for Henry James's life of William Wetmore Story, a complimentary memoir, written at the request of the family, in which the author avoided the embarrassment of facing up to his subject's bad sculpture and poetry by a colorful evocation of his background, including the Boston of his origin. Adams saw much more in this than James had ever intended. He professed to find in the picture of Boston all the ignorance and innocence of a small, closed, parochial society that had been blind enough to believe that a Story could sculpt or a Sumner legislate. It gave him the point from which to start his own *Education*.

It is less the story of an education than the story of the purported failure of one. Adams contends that his family background, his schooling, even his experiences in political and diplomatic circles, in no way prepared him for life in the second half of the nineteenth century. When he and his parents returned to the United States from London in 1868, they were as much strangers in their native land, he claimed, as if they had been Tyrian traders from Gibraltar in the year 1000 B.C. But this, he should in fairness have conceded, was not so much the fault of Harvard or of Boston society, or even of the Adams family, as it was the fault of the raging speed of change in his century. Grant, the new president in 1869, was not, according to Adams, a thinking man, but a simple energy. To achieve worldly success in his era, very little in the way of education was needed. But was worldly success the only kind of success? Because a tycoon had not been educated, was education useless? Adams never convinces us that he would have been willing to scrap the least part of his own maligned education.

Having made his basic point that he was not educated by any of his supposedly educating experiences, Adams proceeds to outline the kind of quasi-education that he received through a series of disillusionments. As a boy he had regarded Senator Charles Sumner as a great statesman and friend; in later years he found him a vain and malicious old peacock. In the early London days he had been convinced that Lord Palmerston was bent on the destruction of the American union and that Gladstone favored the North; later he discovered that just the opposite was true. Friends turned out to be

31

enemies; enemies, friends. Even in the world of art there was no certainty. No expert could tell him whether or not the supposed Raphael sketch that he had bought in London was genuine.

Adams tells the story of each disillusionment entertainingly enough, but in the illusionless world in which we live, we may find his surprise a bit naive. It does not seem to us in the least astonishing that a statesman should say one thing, intend another, and desire a third. Self-interest is so taken for granted that we require our most eminent citizens to sell their stocks before serving in the president's cabinet, and, as for art, we should simply shrug in amusement if it turned out that the roof of the Sistine Chapel had been painted by Boldini.

Finally, in the *Education*, the "uneducated" author, on the threshold of old age, amalgamates his own laws of the sequence of human events with those of the physical sciences to deduce a "dynamic theory" of history that is not taken seriously by either scientists or historians today.

If, then, Adams' claim that he was never educated is simply a paradox for the sake of argument, if his disillusionments strike us as naive, and if his dynamic theory is without validity, wherein lies the greatness of the book? It lies, I submit, in the extraordinarily vivid sense conveyed to the reader of history being formed under his eyes, in the crystallization of the myriad shapes of the twentieth century out of the simple substance of the eighteenth. I know of no other autobiography (as I shall impenitently insist on calling it) which conveys anything like the same effect. And in no other of his writings does Adams more luminously demonstrate what Henry James called "his rich and ingenious mind, his great resources of contemplation, resignation, speculation."

The first chapter introduces us immediately to the philosophic distinction between unity and multiplicity on which the whole work rests. The ordered world of the Federalist era is exemplified by the Adamses and their spare, dignified house in Quincy with its Stuart portraits, family Bibles, and silver mugs, its mementos of Bunker Hill and air of republican simplicity. Surely, this is unity which must have emanated from a single substance, which must radiate a supreme being's will. And the opulent, plush, crowded world of the Brookses in Boston, on the distaff side, with all its tassels and bric-a-brac, its State Street commercialism, must be multiplicity. Is it not town against country, the mad many against the wholesome one? But Adams can spin this wheel so it stops where he wants, and he can make us see each world in terms of the other even at the expense of contradicting himself: "The double exterior nature gave life its relative values. Winter and summer, cold and heat, town and country, force and freedom, marked two modes of life and thought, balanced like lobes of the brain. Town was winter confinement, school, rule, discipline; straight, gloomy streets, piled with six feet of snow in the middle; frosts that made the snow sing under wheels or runners; thaws when the streets became dangerous to cross; society of uncles, aunts, and cousins who expected children to behave themselves, and who were not always gratified; above all else, winter represented the desire to escape and go free. Town was restraint, law, unity. Country, only seven miles away, was liberty, diversity, outlawry, the endless delight of mere sense impressions given by nature for nothing, and breathed by boys without knowing it."

Now follows the unforgettable picture of John Quincy Adams taking his grandson to school. Adams, at six, on a visit to Quincy, had refused to go, and his mother, embarrassed to exercise discipline in her father-in-law's house, was giving in to him when suddenly the door to the ex-president's library opened, and the old man came slowly down the stairs. "Putting on his hat, he took the boy's hand without a word and walked with him, paralyzed by awe, up the road to the town." Not till they had traversed almost a mile on the hot morning did the grandfather release his hand. But Adams did not resent this treatment. "With a certain maturity of mind, the child must have recognized that the President, though a tool of tyranny, had done his disreputable work with a certain intelligence. He had shown no temper, no irritation, no personal feeling, and had made no display of force. Above all, he had held his tongue. During their long walk he had said nothing; he had uttered no syllable of revolting cant about the duty of obedience and the wickedness of resistance to law; he had shown no concern in the matter; hardly even a consciousness of the boy's existence. Probably his mind at that moment was actually troubling itself little about his grandson's iniquities, and much about the iniquities of President Polk, but the boy could scarcely at that age feel the whole satisfaction of thinking that President Polk was to be the vicarious victim of his own sins, and he gave his grandfather credit for intelligent silence. For this forbearance he felt instinctive respect. He admitted force as a form of right; he admitted even temper, under protest; but the seeds of a moral education would at that moment have fallen on the stoniest soil in Quincy, which is, as every one knows, the stoniest glacial and tidal drift known in any Puritan land."

This quotation gives the flavor of the book. We travel through the nineteenth century with a guide who is a good deal less detached than he claims, who is almost at times romantic, almost at times passionate. It is a unique fusion of history and memoir. We see the century growing more diverse and chaotic until it becomes terrifying, but always in the foreground, shrugging, gesticulating, chuckling, at times scolding, is the neat, bustling figure of our impatient but illuminating observer. He can stretch his imagination to any limit, but not his tolerance or his personality. He ends where he began, an aristocrat, a gentleman, a bit of a voyeur. The fixed referent of Henry Adams holds the book together even more than the constant pairing off of unity with multiplicity. At times it almost seems as if Adams himself, cool, rational, skeptical, were the one, and observed mankind, moving at a giddy rate of acceleration toward nothingness, the many. Only in the very end, when the observer disappears into the theorist and the memoir into a theory, does multiplicity at last prevail. One's trouble in reading the *Education* is that as one moves from unity to multiplicity, the story inevitably loses its character and vividness. Most of the memorable passages are from the earlier chapters.

One remembers particularly, after the walk with the grandfather, the desperate snow fight on the Common between the Latin School and the Boston roughs and blackguards, the charm, ignorance, and mindlessness of the handsome Virginians at Harvard, Adams in London exulting over the long-awaited, tragically belated, first victories of the Union armies: "Life never could know more than a single such climax. In that form, education reached its limits. As the first great blows began to fall, one curled up in bed in the silence of night, to listen with incredulous hope. As the huge masses struck, one after another, with the precision of machinery, the opposing mass, the world shivered. Such development of power was unknown. The magnificent resistance and the return shocks heightened the suspense. During the July days Londoners were stupid with unbelief. They were learning from the Yankees how to fight."

Nothing is more notorious about the *Education* than the fact that Marian Adams is never mentioned in it and that the years of her marriage to the author are eliminated. There has been much speculation concerning the reason. An obvious one is that her loss was so terrible that he could not speak or write about her. But this seems inconsistent with his continued lively interest in attractive women and his long romantic friendship with Senator Don Cameron's beautiful wife Elizabeth. Perhaps he simply could not bear to contemplate the attitude toward their marriage which Marian's suicide appeared to imply. The nearest he comes to speaking of her is when he discusses the statue which Augustus St. Gaudens made for him in Rock Creek Cemetery. This, of course, is the famous brooding figure of indeterminate sex which was placed over the inscriptionless grave of Marian Adams and under which Adams himself now lies. Its significance has been much debated, though more in Adams' time than in ours, for enigmatic art was more of a novelty then, but "the peace of God which passeth all understanding" is probably as good an explanation as any.

Adams used to sit by the statue in springtime and listen with acid amusement to the comments of visitors. In a famous and characteristic passage he gave vent to his distaste for the world of his time: "He supposed its meaning to be the one commonplace about it — the oldest idea known to human thought. He knew that if he asked an Asiatic its meaning, not a man, woman, or child from Cairo to Kamtchatka would have needed more than a glance to reply. From the Egyptian Sphinx to the Kamakura Daibuts; from Prometheus to Christ; from Michael Angelo to Shelley, art had wrought on this eternal figure almost as though it had nothing else to say. The interest of the figure was not in its meaning, but in the response of the observer. As Adams sat there, numbers of people came, for the figure seemed to have become a tourist fashion, and all wanted to know its meaning. Most took it for a portrait-statue, and the remnant were vacant-minded in the absence of a personal guide. None felt what would have been a nursery-instinct to a Hindu baby or a Japanese jinricksha-runner. The only exceptions were the clergy, who taught a lesson even deeper. One after another brought companions there, and, apparently fascinated by their own reflection, broke out passionately against the expression they felt in the figure of despair, of atheism, of denial. Like the others, the priest saw only what he brought. Like all the great artists, St. Gaudens held up the mirror and no more. The American layman had lost sight of ideals; the American priest had lost sight of faith. Both were more American than the old, half-witted soldiers who denounced the wasting, on a mere grave, of money which should have been given for drink."

The "education" of Henry Adams might be defined as his own belated conviction that science, for all its achievements, had not resolved the basic mystery of the one and the many, the eternal question of whether the universe is a divine unity or a composite of more than one ultimate substance, a super-sensuous chaos that no single theory can encompass. The only thing of which the author of *Mont-Saint-Michel* and the *Education* could feel absolutely sure was that in the twelfth century man had believed in such a unity and that in the twentieth his less fortunate descendant did not. All Adams could now see in the dark and dangerous era that lay ahead was the seemingly unintelligible interplay of forces.

After finishing the *Education* he devoted himself entirely to trying to make that interplay intelligible. He hoped that it might still be possible to derive some rule from these forces by which he could make a projection of the future. Defining force as anything that helps to do work, and identifying man and nature as forces, he was able to turn history, or social evolution, into a gravitational field in which man and nature constantly acted on and modified each other. The declining force of the church in the past few centuries, for example, gave place to the force of a secular society energized by gunpowder and the compass. In the twentieth century man had to reconcile himself to the loss of the concept of unity and follow the movements of the new forces of nature discovered by experiment. This following would open a new phase in history, the phase of the acceleration of mechanical forces. Adams, spending his mornings at his desk playing with magnets, became obsessed with the vision of human society approaching the ultimate forces with a dizzily accelerating speed, like a comet shooting to the sun.

His writings of this period, "The Rule of Phase Applied to History" (1908) and *A Letter to American Teachers of History* (1910), contain postulations of human life and psychical activity more or less corresponding to the physical phases of solids, liquids, and gases. He finally worked out a mathematical formula based on the law of squares by which he predicted a change of phase (following the human phases of "instinct" and "religion") in 1917 and a breakdown in human thought four years later. All of this is beyond the scope of this essay, but in the opinion of many commentators Adams went hopelessly astray in applying the laws of physics to human events so that his theorizing amounts to little more than brilliant and imaginative fantasy.

It was a waste, unhappily, of valuable energy. Adams' obsession with the mystery of the universe deflected him from the true path on which Mrs. Lodge had set him when they toured the Gothic cathedrals of northern France. Who today would give up *Mont-Saint-Michel* for "Rule of Phase"? With old age he gave in more and more to the nervous habit of questioning everything which had so irritated his friend Justice Oliver Wendell Holmes. The latter wrote this description of him to Lewis Einstein, eight years after Adams' death: "He was very keen and a thinker, but seems to me to have allowed himself to be satisfied too easily that there was no instruction for him in the branches in which he dabbed. When I would step in at his house on the way back from Court and found him playing the old Cardinal, he would spend his energy in pointing out that everything was dust and ashes. Of course one did not yield to the disenchantment, but it required so much counter energy in a man tired with his day's work that I didn't call often. And yet meet him casually on the street and often he was a delightful creation."

Mont-Saint-Michel and the *Education* were both printed privately (in 1904 and 1907 respectively) in large, handsome blue-covered folio editions, one of a hundred and fifty and the other of forty copies, and distributed to friends and a few libraries. Adams did not think the public at large would be interested; he probably thought it was not intellectually ready. He refused to allow an eager young publisher, Ferris Greenslet, from Houghton Mifflin, to tempt him with a contract for the *Education*, but he finally allowed the same firm to bring out an edition of *Mont-Saint-Michel* which appeared, with an introduction by Ralph Adams Cram, in 1913. One wonders if he would have been altogether pleased had he foreseen the enormous popularity that both books would enjoy in the next half century. Would he have been gratified to find himself a "best seller" in an age whose intellectual taste he despised?

I believe that Adams always misconceived his principal talent. He wanted the recognition of scientists for his theories in a field where he was not equipped to make any serious contribution. The picture of Adams, the descendant of presidents, a kind of early American "Everyman," a survival from the Civil War in the day of the automobile, traveling from one end of the globe to the other in quest of the absolute, pausing before Buddhas and dynamos, has so caught the imagination of the academic community that his biography, which he wrote as well as lived, has become, so to speak, one of his works, and his most fantastic speculations the subjects of serious theses. Yet to me his primary contributions to our literature were aesthetic. He is far closer to Whitman and Melville than to Bancroft or Prescott, and he is not at all close to Einstein.

In history he went as far as could be gone on the basic presumption, later repudiated by himself, that the study of trade, diplomacy, and politics can be made to reveal the sequence of human events. No historian has unraveled with more illuminating clarity the exchange of thought in chancellories, the effects of embargoes, and the influences of electorates on legislators and administrators. If Adams' historical writing leans to the austere, it is because he

39

was determined not to be sidetracked by the quaint, the picturesque, the sensational, or the merely entertaining. Although he denied this from time to time, as when he wrote his publishers that he had given the public a "full dose" of Andrew Jackson because of its "undue interest" in that soldier and statesman, his denial is not convincing, for nobody could think that the portrait of Jackson in the *History* is more than a minimal sketch.

Adams gave up writing American history because he did not believe, after long consideration of what he had done, that he had made any really significant contribution to the long quest for cause and effect. Yet, when he turned from the austerity of historical writing to the looser and more copious field of the novel, he discovered that he did not have the kind of imagination that operated much more easily without limitations of fact. The historian is only too evident in *Democracy* and *Esther*. Both tales are confined to the bare bones of their situations. There is almost no detail of background, and the characters are analyzed only insofar as necessary for us to understand their plotted actions. As in seventeenth-century French fiction, we are confined to essentials. Adams may have considered that in depicting his senator as a monster he was allowing himself a riot of indulgence, but Ratcliffe is given the smallest possible crime to justify his classification as villain.

It is interesting in this respect to contrast his mind with that of Henry James, a lifelong friend whose fiction Adams consistently admired. No two minds could have been more different. As Leon Edel has pointed out, Adams always sought a generalization while James sought to particularize. Adams wanted to know the law of the universe, while James was studying the effect of Paris on a single American soul. Yet each man appreciated the other. Adams loved the subtlety of James's characterizations, and James admired the sweep of Adams' reaching. James, however, would not have approved of Adams' experimentation with the novel form. To him the art of fiction was only for the totally dedicated. We know that he read *Democracy* and said of it that, despite the coarseness of its satire, it was so good that it was a pity it was not better, but he did not know that Adams had written it.

Adams did not find the medium of expression best adapted to his talents until he left the world behind and went to the Pacific with John La Farge. In Tahiti he explored the reconciliation of instinct with logic in his history of the island. There was no even seeming sequence of events to be derived from economics or diplomacy. He had to find it in legends and customs inextricably tied up with the emotions which, as a historian in the older sense, he had tried to eliminate from the field of observed phenomena. The experiment was not a success, but it was a rehearsal of what he was next to do when he came to the Gothic cathedrals of France. "Putting the feeling back" in the stones of Chartres was his goal there, and he attained it. He then proceeded to expand this goal, in the *Education*, to putting the feeling back into his own life and into the contemporary history of the United States and wrote one of the monuments of American literature.

It is not to denigrate the earlier work of Adams to say that *Mont-Saint-Michel* and the *Education* represent the finest flowering of his mind. The biographies and the *History* are not only valuable in themselves; they were indispensable preliminaries. But one may regret that Adams did not more fully recognize his own major phase. He was always determined to be valued for something other than his best.

The great bulk of his correspondence, filling three volumes, shows this. Some of the letters, particularly those from the Pacific, are as brilliant and evocative as John La Farge's water colors of the same subject. But through the ones that deal with social and political life the shrill, constantly repeated strain of dramatic and rhetorical pessimism becomes a great bore. One wonders why

Adams thought that it would divert his correspondents. And then, too, he seems to take a perverse pleasure in *not* giving descriptions of people and events that one knows he could describe incomparably. Perhaps it was because all his friends knew the same people and events, but to the modern reader it is like reading Saint-Simon with the characterizations removed. If Adams had only had a correspondent on the moon to whom he had had to give an impression of our planet, a niece in space, he might have been the greatest letter writer in American literature.

His last book, *The Life of George Cabot Lodge*, was published in 1911. It was a memoir that he had written about the senator's son, "Bay," a poet who had died prematurely two years before. The memoir had been written at the request of Senator Lodge and given to him to publish or not as he pleased. It is a tactful and charming piece in which the narrative is largely used to string together quotations from the young man's letters. This is not because Adams was embarrassed by a task that he could not well refuse. He enormously liked Bay Lodge and evidently admired his poetry. But he was by nature too reticent for this kind of eulogy. Perhaps it was just as well. The letters reveal a young man whose talent must have been more in his flaming good looks and enthusiasm than in any originality of imagination or poetic aptitude. Bay Lodge's idealism and aspiration seem to have charmed the aging Adams. They went to the theater together in Paris and discussed ideas for Lodge's plays. They formed together a fanciful political party called the Conservative Christian Anarchists. Lodge was a rebel against Boston society, but he expressed his rebellion largely by appearance, in the manner of some youths today. He wore a huge black hat and gold watch around his neck and let his hair grow long. At least he was going to *look* like an artist. Perhaps he fascinated Adams because he was so exactly his opposite. Adams always dressed and acted the conservative, but his black frock coat covered the heart of a poet.

In 1912 Adams reserved passage from New York to Europe on what would have been the second voyage of the *Titanic*. This brought the disaster of her maiden trip very close to him, and he was much affected. No doubt it seemed even more a symbol to him than it did to others of the disastrous acceleration of science of our century. A week later, he was stricken with a slight stroke. Despite his conviction that he would not survive, he recovered full use of his mind and body, but it became necessary for him to have somebody to supervise the details of his housekeeping, and Aileen Tone, a beautiful young woman who was the friend of two of his nieces, undertook the job. She became his secretary, companion, and adopted niece, and remained with him until his death six years later. As a member of the Schola Cantorum she had learned piano arrangements for old French songs which she used to sing to Adams and his friends. He found in their atonalities a possibility of recapturing the music of the twelfth-century poems that he so loved. In his letters to Miss Tone, during her brief visits away to look after her mother, he made constant references to medieval France, addressing her as "Comtesse Soeur" (as Richard I had addressed his sister) and describing himself as "Robin," the shepherd in a chante-fable. As the end approached, he lived more and more in his chosen century.

The last year was darkened by bad war news. It seemed the long anticipated Götterdämmerung. Adams continued, however, to read, to study, to write letters and see friends. Miss Tone took him for daily drives, read to him and helped, as he put it, to keep him alive. The end came in the winter of 1918.

His family discovered the manuscript of a curious and beautiful poem in Adams' wallet. It was entitled "Prayer to the Virgin of Chartres" and was published with some of his correspondence in

Letters to a Niece in 1920. Because of the depth of its mystical feeling, some of Adams' friends, particularly Mrs. Winthrop Chanler, to whom he had shown the poem in his lifetime, thought that he might have been turning toward Roman Catholicism. But if there is religious feeling in the "Prayer," it is heresy even by the most liberal standards of the Church today. The poem very neatly synthesizes Adams' philosophy.

He sees himself as appearing before his "Gracious Lady" to ask her aid, as simple and humble as his counterpart of seven hundred years before, in the year 1200. He identifies himself with Mary's worshipers throughout medieval history: he has prayed before her portal with Abélard and sung the "Ave Maris Stella" with Saint Bernard of Clairvaux. However, for all his devotion, he recognizes that Mary has always been helpless to help him, even back in the days of her greatness when Chartres was built:

> For centuries I brought you all my cares,
>   And vexed you with the murmurs of a child;
> You heard the tedious burden of my prayers;
>   You could not grant them, but at least you smiled.

Because Mary is impotent in the affairs of men, Adams, or Everyman, the "English scholar with a Norman name," abandons her to seek the Father, as Christ himself did, when he went about his Father's business. In this there may be a reference to Saint Thomas Aquinas restoring the Trinity to the center of creation and dethroning the Virgin. In looking for the Father Adams only loses the Mother. The Church of Saint Thomas, without the love and laughter of Mary, without the illogic of her abounding grace, is a sterile combination of cold virtue and damnation.

Adams now visualizes himself as crossing the Atlantic to the New World with a greedy band of Europeans, intent on the plunder of America. He has turned his back not only on the Virgin, the Mother, but on God the Father, too. In the secular society that man

44

is now creating, there is no room for a deity. If man is to revere anything, it must be himself alone, even if that self is mortal without a soul to survive its body.

> And now we are the Father, with our brood,
> Ruling the Infinite, not Three but One;
> We made our world and saw that it was good;
> Ourselves we worship, and we have no Son.

But this independence is illusory. Man discovers that there is still a god to worship, not a just god, like the Father, or a loving and merciful one, like the Virgin, but one that is only force, primal force. The meter changes, and the "Prayer to the Virgin" is interrupted by the "Prayer to the Dynamo," the last of the strange orisons that humanity has "wailed."

Whether the primal force is matter or mind, the only thing man knows about it is that it is blind and cannot respond to prayer. Man and force, lords of space, may both be approaching some end or limit at a terrifying rate of acceleration. It remains only for man to wrest the secret from the atom, but here Adams, with a prescience that is more alarming in the 1970's than it may have been in 1920, sees the hollowest of victories. The victor over the atom will have little on which to congratulate himself.

> Seize, then, the Atom! rack his joints!
> Tear out of him his secret spring!
> Grind him to nothing! — though he points
> To us, and his life-blood anoints
> Me — the dead Atom-King!

The poem now reverts to the form of the prayer to the Virgin. Adams, or Everyman, has come again to seek the help of the helpless Mary. He has no further faith in science and has fled modern man who needs the force of solar systems for his grim play. The latter, too, will find the hopelessness that Adams has found. There

45

is nothing left but the Virgin and the barren consolation that she has to offer.

Does he mean the Virgin or his idea of the Virgin or the medieval concept of the Virgin? It seems to me that he means a fusion of the last two. Adams seems to be clinging to a faith in his own concept of a historical conception that has no current validity and that must have been only an illusion in the twelfth century. For the Virgin was helpless even then. She did not exist. She was an idea, no more, but such a magnificent idea that she could and can console men who *know* that she was and is only an idea, that, indeed, she is now only the memory of one.

In the end he prays to the Virgin to give him her sight, her knowledge, and her feeling. She must have the strength to help him, he argues, because she has had the strength to endure the failure of the very concept of God. It is on this note of ultimate pessimism that the great pessimist leaves us:

> Help me to feel! not with my insect sense, —
>   With yours that felt all life alive in you;
> Infinite heart beating at your expense;
>   Infinite passion breathing the breath you drew!
>
> Help me to bear! Not my own baby load,
>   But yours; who bore the failure of the light,
> The strength, the knowledge and the thought of God, —
>   The futile folly of the Infinite!

✒ Selected Bibliography

Works of Henry Adams

BIOGRAPHIES

The Life of Albert Gallatin. Philadelphia: Lippincott, 1879.
John Randolph. Boston: Houghton Mifflin, 1882.
The Life of George Cabot Lodge. Boston: Houghton Mifflin, 1911.

HISTORY

History of the United States of America during the First Administration of Thomas Jefferson. 9 vols. New York: Scribner's, 1889–91.
Historical Essays. New York: Scribner's, 1891. (Containing "Captain John Smith," "The Bank of England Restriction," "The Declaration of Paris," "The Legal Tender Act," "The New York Gold Conspiracy," "The Session.")
Memoirs of Arii Taimai of Tahiti. Paris: Privately published, 1901.
Mont-Saint-Michel and Chartres. Boston: Houghton Mifflin, 1913.
The Degradation of the Democratic Dogma. New York: Macmillan, 1919. (Containing "The Rule of Phase Applied to History," *A Letter to American Teachers of History*.)

AUTOBIOGRAPHY

The Education of Henry Adams. Boston: Houghton Mifflin, 1918.

NOVELS

Democracy: An American Novel. (Anonymous.) Leisure Hour Series No. 112. New York: Henry Holt, 1880.
Esther: A Novel. (Pseudonym, Frances Snow Compton.) American Novel Series No. 3. New York: Henry Holt, 1884.

VERSE

Letters to a Niece and Prayer to the Virgin of Chartres. Boston: Houghton Mifflin, 1920.

BOOKS EDITED

Essays in Anglo-Saxon Law. Boston: Little, Brown, 1876.
The Writings of Albert Gallatin. 3 vols. Philadelphia: Lippincott, 1879.

47

LETTERS

Letters of Henry Adams 1858–1891, edited by Worthington C. Ford. Boston: Houghton Mifflin, 1930.

Letters of Henry Adams 1892–1918, edited by Worthington C. Ford. Boston: Houghton Mifflin, 1938.

Henry Adams and His Friends, edited (with a biographical introduction) by Harold Dean Cater. Boston: Houghton Mifflin, 1947.

CURRENT AMERICAN REPRINTS

The Degradation of the Democratic Dogma. New York: Torch (Harper and Row). $2.75.

Democracy. New York: Signet (New American Library). $.50.

The Education of Henry Adams. New York: Modern Library (Random House). $2.45. Boston: Sentry (Houghton Mifflin). $2.65.

History of the United States (abbreviated). Englewood Cliffs, N.J.: Spectrum (Prentice-Hall). $2.95.

Mont-Saint-Michel and Chartres. New York: Mentor (New American Library). $.75. New York: Anchor (Doubleday). $1.45. Boston: Sentry. $2.45.

Biographical and Critical Studies

Adams, James Truslow. *Henry Adams*. New York: Albert and Charles Boni, 1933.

Blackmur, Richard P. "The Novels of Henry Adams," *Sewanee Review*, 51:281–304 (Spring 1943).

Brooks, Van Wyck. *The Confident Years 1885–1915*. New York: Dutton, 1952.

Chanler, Mrs. Winthrop. *Roman Spring*. Boston: Little, Brown, 1936.

Jordy, William H. *Henry Adams, Scientific Historian*. New Haven, Conn.: Yale University Press, 1952.

Levenson, J. C. *The Mind and Art of Henry Adams*. Boston: Houghton Mifflin, 1957.

Samuels, Ernest. *The Young Henry Adams*. Cambridge, Mass.: Harvard University Press, 1948.

————. *Henry Adams: The Middle Years*. Cambridge, Mass.: Harvard University Press, 1958.

————. *Henry Adams: The Major Phase*. Cambridge, Mass.: Harvard University Press, 1964.

Stevenson, Elizabeth. *Henry Adams*. New York: Macmillan, 1955.